Otters
For Kids

Amazing Animal Books
For Young Readers

By
Rachel Smith

Mendon Cottage Books
JD-Biz Corp Publishing

Read More Amazing Animal Books

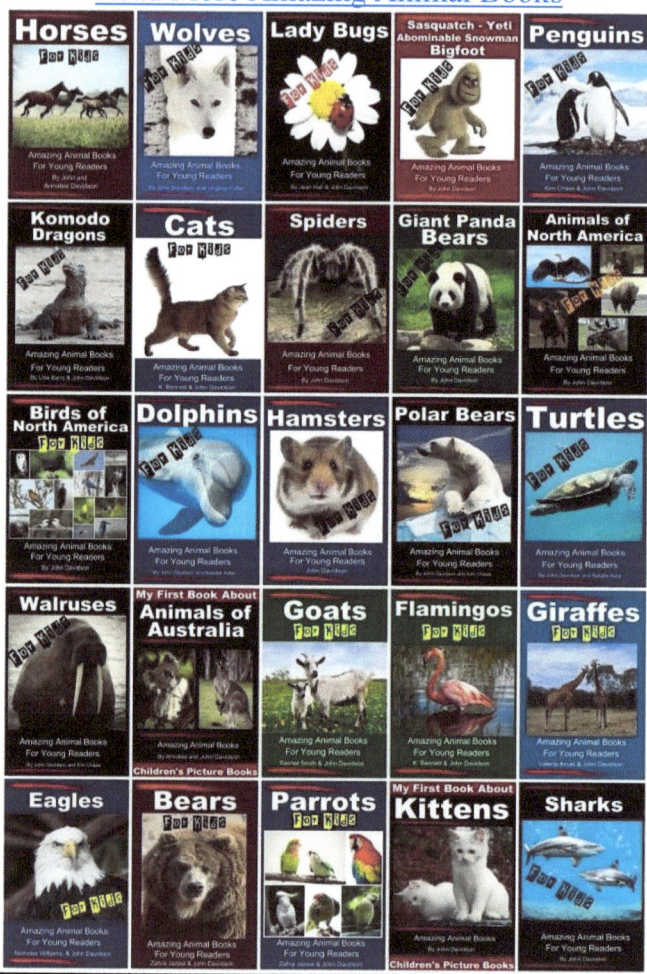

Purchase at Amazon.com

Table of Contents

Introduction

Otters have long been a favorite animal of many people. They live throughout the world, and populate the world of fiction as well.

A popular British series, Redwall, uses them a lot as good guys. Another place that the otter shows up, is in the book Wind in the Willows, which is a beloved story about a toad, an otter, and other creatures.

The otter has always come across to humans as cute, as well as entertaining. They are fast swimmers, and have been popular on the internet for their habit of holding on to each others' paws when out at sea or something of the sort.

But there's more to otters than just being cute or being a good character in a book. Not only is there more than one kind of otter, there are also many different facts about them most people don't know.

Read on and find out!

What is an otter?

An otter is a member of the subfamily Lutrinae. They are somewhat closely related to weasels and their relatives. They come from the same family. However, there are a lot of things about otters that distinguish them from their cousins.

Two giant otters.

For one thing, otters are all aquatic, semi-aquatic, or marine animals. This means that their lives revolve a lot around being in the water. Different types of otters live different lives, but one thing they all have in common is their ability to swim.

They all have long, thin bodies, webbed paws, sharp claws, and most of them have long, muscular tails.

Otters are all carnivorous. This means that they eat meat, and can't survive on things like vegetables or plants. Otters live in homes called dens or couches. A male is called a dog, a female is called a bitch, and a baby is called a pup.

They are called a romp, bevy, or family (among other names) in groups. And there is a good reason for this: otters stick together in families.

When a pup is born, it can count on both its mother and its father to take care of it, as well as older siblings. A mother otter is only pregnant for about two to three months, less than a third of how long a human mother must be pregnant before the baby can be born. Baby otters can leave the den after only a month, and after two months they can usually swim. A pup will stay with its family for at least a year.

Otters live up to sixteen years. Females are ready to have babies by two years old, and males by three.

They hunt for various kinds of foods, from crabs to fish. An otter that lives in the water near-constantly has to eat a lot of food to produce enough heat to survive in the water, as water typically leeches heat from the body.

Many types of otters live in or near water; however, the river otters don't.

While many adhere to family groups or something similar, there are also otters that are alone. It depends on the species involved.

What kinds of otters are there?

There are a lot of kinds of otters. Some are tiny, like the Oriental small-clawed otter. Others are enormous, such as sea otters and giant otters.

Some Asian small-clawed otters.

You can group them into a few groups: the group including the river otters and the marine otter. The giant otter, which stands on its own; the group of European otters, as well as the extinct Japanese otter and a number of prehistoric otters, and then the group of African and Oriental otters.

Behaviors, water time, and other things set apart each group. It's important to know that every otter has its differences, especially in habitat.

Since they all belong to the same subfamily, however, there is less difference than there would be examining the entire family they are in.

Where do otters live?

Otters live all over the world. Some of the largest kinds live in South America, whereas other smaller otters live in places like Africa and Asia.

A group of European otters.

As mentioned before, there used to be a Japanese-native otter, but it was hunted out. Japan's rapid modernization had a strong effect on the animals that lived there.

There are also otters that live in North America, in the rivers. These are the kinds American children are probably most familiar with. Then there's the European otter, which is the kind European children are probably most familiar with.

Otherwise, otters are a varied bunch. They live throughout the world, but they don't live in places like the Arctic or Antarctica. It's too cold for them there, and they wouldn't survive.

Most otters live near water. River otters are a bit of the exception, as they might not live too close to the water. On the other end, sea otters spend almost all of their time in the water.

With their webbed paws and streamlined bodies, the otters are well suited to almost any place with moving water and plentiful fish and such.

The history of otters and humans

The history of otters and humans is not necessarily a happy one. It would be great to be able to say that otters and humans have always gotten along and lived alongside each other in peace, but that would be inaccurate.

A smooth-coated otter.

The otter has fur that was considered valuable and stylish in Europe. This means that when otters were discovered in North America, they were heavily hunted. There were so many otters caught for their fur that the remaining population made making a profit (the money made from selling furs minus the costs of getting the furs) impossible. It was only in 1911 that a treaty was made to protect otters in America.

The otter is still hunted in places such as Southeast Asia, as many places throughout Asia still place a great value on otter fur. They are used as mitten, belts, great robes-- all manner of things.

Because of all this hunting, in many places otters are endangered, and especially in Southeast Asia.

However, the otter does have some positive relationships with humans. In Bangladesh, which is in Asia, many fishers trained smooth-coated otters to fish for them. This used to be much more widespread; nowadays, it's only practiced by one area in Bangladesh.

Otters in mythology show up in several places. For one, there's the Norse dwarf Otr, who frequently disguised himself as an otter. Korean mythology says those who see an otter will attract rain clouds. Native American groups (some, not all) have the otter as a totem animal.

Japanese mythology is where it gets interesting; in many areas of Japan, it is believed that otters can turn into beautiful women, as well as children, who are wearing checkered clothes. They will lure men and eat them.

This is somewhat similar to foxes and raccoon-dogs. However, the otter has other tales in Japan: turning into a monk, or possessing people. It's said that those possessed by otters will lose power and stamina.

However, most otters are never this scary, as long as you respect that they are wild animals and not potential pets.

European otters

European otters are literally called, in their scientific name, Lutra Lutra. So, basically 'Otter Otter.' This is the first otter the Western scientific community knew about.

A European otter.

This type of otter is a river otter, and is, more accurately, often called the Eurasian otter, meaning that it lives in both Asia and Europe. It also lives in North Africa. It might be extinct in Switzerland and Liechtenstein, two small countries in the heart of Europe, but it is doing very well in Latvia (a small Eastern European country), and in parts of the UK and Ireland.

Thanks to pesticides and such, it is much harder to find an otter in England; but in Scotland and Northern Ireland, there are a lot more otters. This type of otter is especially common in Shetland (which is a part of the UK) and most densely populated in Ireland.

It can be found in southern parts of Italy, and as far East as South Korea. However, it is endangered in South Korea.

So, what makes the European otter the European otter?

For one thing, they are solitary creatures. European otters are territorial, which means that they mark their area and won't allow other otters into the area most of the time. The one exception is when a female otter has pups; the male will let her stay in a part of his territory, but he won't help with the pups or have anything to do with them.

This is because European otters only defend their territory against other European otters of the same sex. They aren't concerned about otters of the opposite sex.

They can live either in the sea or freshwater, though they are more adapted to river living. If a European otter stays in the ocean, it still needs to go to freshwater to clean its fur. European otters eat a lot of fish and things like crustaceans, birds, and even young beavers. They will tend towards fish if they can, though.

European otters mate and have babies any time of the year; unlike some animals, they don't have mating seasons.

They hunt through sight and touch for sure, and there's speculation that they may be able to smell underwater, a feat accomplished by few mammals.

In England, this kind of otter was nearly wiped out from every county; through years of hard work, banning harmful pesticides, improving water quality, and other such things, there are now otters in every county in England.

In Hong Kong, it's a protected species.

North American river otters

The North American river otter is also known as the common otter, at least in America and possibly Canada.

North American river otter.

River otters are semi-aquatic, meaning that they are equally able to function on land as in water. This also means that they don't swim in saltwater, though river otters will live at or in swamps, lakes, rivers, and all kinds of freshwater bodies of water.

It has a thick coat of fur, so it can survive in the water; also, its fur is water-repellant, sort of like a duck's feathers are. This protects it from getting too cold; otters don't have much body fat, so they need to make up for it by keeping the chill-inducing water out of their fur.

River otters have been mostly in decline for the past 200 years; at some points in history, due to habitat loss and hunting, they came near being endangered. However, they are no long endangered, and enjoy a good population throughout North America.

They eat mostly fish, and they prefer it that way, though they will eat crayfish, birds, and other animals that are easy enough prey. They like the fish that are easiest to catch, so slow-swimming fish are much more likely to be eaten by otters, unless there are not enough of them.

However, in some areas, crayfish are much more plentiful than fish, so river otters will eat many of those instead. And some of the birds these otters may eat include ducks, such as the mallard or the ruddy duck.

In the water, there's almost nothing that hunts the North American river otter; killer whales or alligators will eat them, but they don't tend to exist in the same areas much. However, on land, there are many more predators for the river otter: the black bear, the mountain lion, the bobcat, the gray wolf, and even domesticated dogs.

The majority of otters who die of non-old-age related reasons, however, don't die at the hands of animals. Instead, otters tend to be hurt by humans, whether by getting caught in fishing traps, being illegally hunted, or through habitat destruction.

Habitat destruction and water pollution was a huge problem for the otters by the early 1900s; however, a lot of laws have been passed in both Canada and America to help restore good aquatic habitats and nowadays, this type of otter is not endangered, though its range isn't as wide as it used to be.

Smooth-coated otters

Smooth-coated otters, as mentioned before, were once trained throughout Southeast Asia and South Asia to fish for humans. Now, it only takes place in one area in Bangladesh.

A smooth-coated otter.

Hailing from as far apart as Iraq to India to Vietnam, the smooth-coated otter is so called because it has a smoother and shorter coat of fur than most other otters.

This type of otter has a nose shaped sort of like a diamond, and it tends to be a little bigger than the average otter. It also has a flattened tail, whereas most otters have rounded tails. They also have webbed feet, with sharp claws.

Smooth-coated otters require freshwater. They will live almost anywhere there is freshwater, such as rice paddies and streams and the like. If another form of otter is there, however, they will move to a better spot. This type of otter also does well in the ocean, but still needs freshwater to drink and swim in to clean their fur. They absolutely can't survive without it.

Interestingly, there is a population of these otters isolated in Iran in the swamplands. Other than that, it pretty strictly lives in South and Southeast Asia.

Since they are social otters, smooth-coated otters hunt in groups. They also are diurnal, like humans, which means that they are active during the day. They do rest at about midday, however, when it's hottest. This type of otter doesn't prefer cavorting about at night.

One way these otters communicate with each other and other animals is through scent. In their tails, these otters have scent glands (glands are organs that release hormones or secretions, in this case, a scent) at the base of their tail. They use these in an action called sprainting; they mark their area so that other animals stay out of it.

They also make noises to communicate, ranging from whistles and chirps to wails.

Smooth-coated otters live in dens; these can be constructed among dense trees and plants, around boulders, and under tree roots, for a few examples. This is where they sleep.

Sometimes, this kind of otter will make a holt. This is similar to a beaver's dam, and has a similar layout; there are hidden entrances, generally underwater, and is somewhat large. These homes are more permanent than the dens they make elsewhere.

Smooth-coated otters eat mostly fish, though they will eat reptiles, crustaceans, small mammals, birds, and so on.

When they hunt together, they've been known to form a v-shape as a group, and scare the fish so that they are easier to catch. These otters will usually hunt with the largest kind in the middle.

This kind of otter will mate either throughout the year, or, in areas that depend on seasonal water, around a time that would be good for the young. A mother smooth-coated otter will typically give birth to four or more, though more is rare. The pups are blind and helpless, but within ten days they are able to see.

The pups end up being weaned from their mother (meaning they don't need her milk anymore) once they're two to three months old. A smooth-coated otter becomes an adult at about one year of age. They are able to have their own babies at about two or three years of age.

However, there are problems facing this kind of otter. There are many hydroelectric (meaning making electricity through the power of water) projects, land reclamation, marsh draining, and other things that contribute to a lack of habitat for the smooth-coated otter. Also, because of the larger and larger populations of the Asian countries they live in, and the related high levels of poverty, the otters find they have to contend with poverty-stricken people who use the natural resources to support themselves. There is also intentional trapping of these otters in South Asia.

In Iraq, there was a lot of fear that the former tyrant, Saddam Hussein, had caused the extinction of the Iraqi smooth-coated otter through draining the area that they lived in. However, nowadays there seems to be evidence that they are still around.

Marine otters

Marine otters are incredibly rare. Not as much is known about them as most other kinds of otters; their name, at least, their scientific name, means 'marine cat.' And they do resemble cats.

However, the important thing to know about marine otters is that they are not sea otters, and are in fact very different from their cousins.

They live in South America, along the coast of Peru, Chile, and the lowest parts of Argentina. However, they have been seen as far away as the Falkland Islands. They tend towards habitats that are exposed to wind and swells of water, seeming not to like quiet inland areas. Instead, they seem to be most open to danger, in comparison to other otters.

This is because the marine otter, despite its name, does not spend a lot of time in the water. In fact, out of all otters, it spends the least amount of time in water.

It's also the second smallest kind of otter; only the Oriental small-clawed otter is smaller.

It has dark brown fur on top, and a lighter color underneath. However, it also has gray guard hairs, and its fur is more coarse and tough than a sea otter's.

It's believed that they feed off of fish, crustaceans, and other sea creatures. No one knows with absolute certainty, however, as they are hard to track and hard to observe.

No one knows how many are left. They are protected under the law of the countries they live in primarily, though they were once the target of fur-hunters and fishers.

Sea otters

The sea otter is one of the heaviest members of the weasel family, despite being quite small. Unlike its cousin the marine otter, it spends most of its life in the sea.

A sea otter.

Many creatures that live in the sea, such as seals and whales, depend on blubber to keep themselves warm. Not the sea otter; instead, it has the thickest fur coat in the animal kingdom.

It lives in between the Western and Eastern coasts of the Pacific Ocean, generally more towards the North. It eats invertebrates (creatures without vertebrae, which means they have no spine) and some kinds of fish.

This otter is considered one of the more smart animals in the animal kingdom. This is because they use tools, namely, rocks, to open things like clams. The sea otter dives down to grab things such as fish, urchins, and other sea life, and it eats them.

Sea otters, when sleeping, which they often do in the ocean, have been known to hold hands with other sea otters so they don't get separated.

They mate in a way that the male has more than one female; often, he will bite them on the nose when mating.

The female takes good care of her pups; she licks and grooms them until their fur has so much air in it that the pup floats in the water and can't dive or sink.

The big problem for sea otters, or rather, the two problems, is that they go after fish that humans eat, and they have very beautiful fur. Between the 1700s and up to about 1911, sea otters were hunted without mercy, until there were only about one or two thousand left in the wild, compared to the population before of hundreds of thousands.

Fortunately, this was about the time that people started to care about preserving species, and new programs were put into place to bring back the sea otter. Now, it lives in about two thirds of the places it used to live, though whether or not they will recover their numbers in a world that is constantly overfished is up to debate.

Conclusion

Otters are cute, adorable creatures who survived one of the biggest hunts in the history of the world. They are resilient creatures, and they will probably be around, in some form or another, in the many centuries to come.

As long as people continue their conservation efforts, the otter has nothing to fear.

Author Bio

Rachel Smith is a young author who enjoys animals. Once, she had a rabbit who was very nervous, and chewed through her leash and tried to escape. She's also had several pet mice, who were the funniest little animals to watch. She lives in Ohio with her family and writes in her spare time.

Our books are available at
1. Amazon.com

2. Barnes and Noble

3. Itunes

4. Kobo

5. Smashwords

6. Google Play Books

Publisher

JD-Biz Corp

P O Box 374

Mendon, Utah 84325

http://www.jd-biz.com/

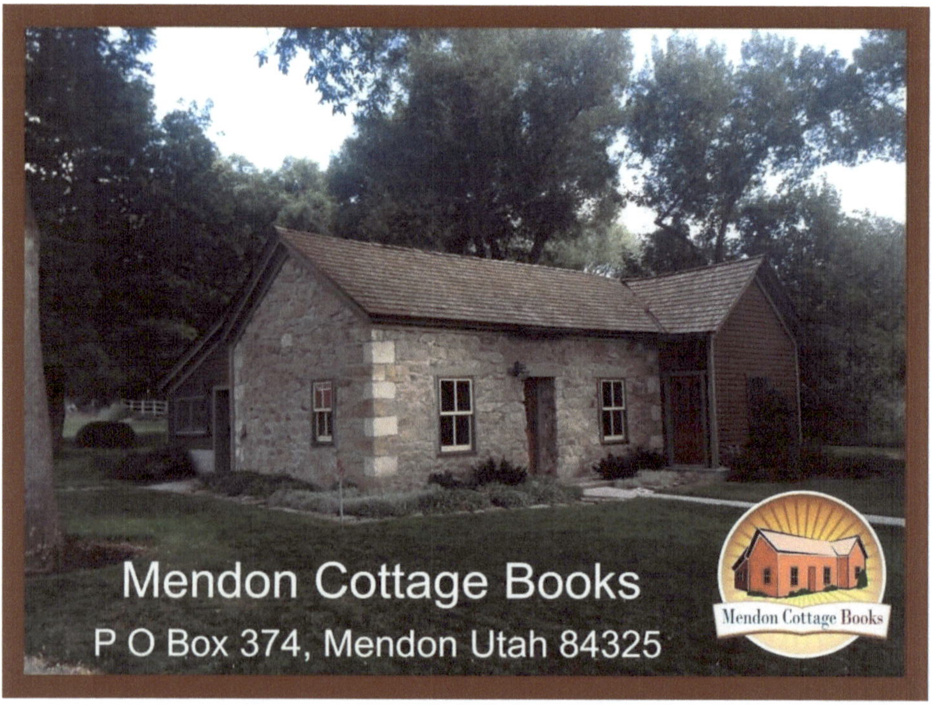

Mendon Cottage Books

P O Box 374, Mendon Utah 84325

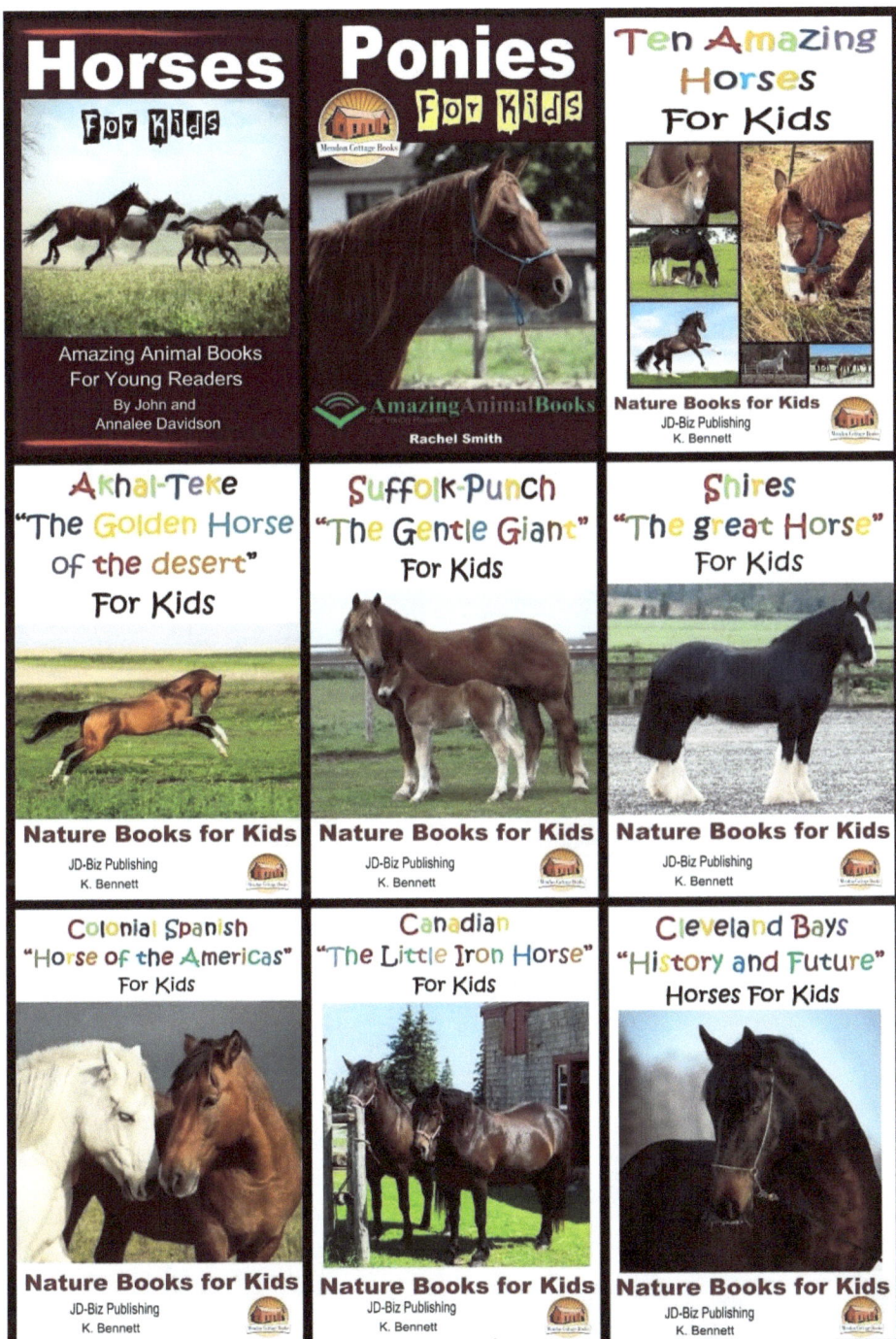

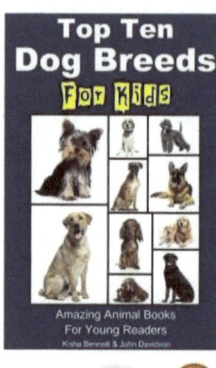

Top Ten Dog Breeds For Kids
Amazing Animal Books For Young Readers
Kisha Bennett & John Davidson

German Shepherds
Dog Books for Kids
K. Bennett

Bulldogs
Dog Books for Kids
K. Bennett

Dachshund
Dog Books for Kids
K. Bennett

Poodles
Dog Books for Kids
K. Bennett

Labrador Retrievers
Dog Books for Kids
K. Bennett

Rottweilers
Dog Books for Kids
K. Bennett

Boxers
Dog Books for Kids
K. Bennett

Golden Retrievers
Dog Books for Kids
K. Bennett

Puppies
Dog Books For Kids
Amazing Animal Books
By John Davidson

Beagles
Dog Books for Kids
K. Bennett

Yorkshire Terriers
Dog Books for Kids
K. Bennett

Dogs
Top Ten Dog Breeds For Kids
Amazing Animal Books For Young Readers
Zahra Jazeel & John Davidson

Cats For Kids
Amazing Animal Books For Young Readers
K. Bennett & John Davidson

Foxes For Kids
Amazing Animal Books For Young Readers
Zahra Jazeel & John Davidson

Wolves For Kids
Amazing Animal Books For Young Readers
By John Davidson and Virginia Fidler

www.ingramcontent.com/pod-product-compliance
Lightning Source LLC
Chambersburg PA
CBHW050903290526
45792CB00002B/684